ir·rev·o·ca·ble

əˈrevəkəb(ə)l

ir·rev·o·ca·ble

əˈrevəkəb(ə)l

Prayers and Decrees Declared Through Psalm 103

Annice Silimon

Dedication

To all the people of prayer committed to a lifestyle of worship.

Your worship matters.

Using this book is simple…

1.Prayers and decrees to be read, meditated upon, and prayed INTO.

2. Irrevocable is based upon one Psalm--Psalm 103. Do not complicate this, just pray and decree.

3. Add your personal decrees and declarations—make this experience your own.

4. Pray these words over others—sow it forward.

This is a simple labor of love. I simply transcribed a small piece of the heart of GOD concerning you.

The process was an honor. Thank you for journeying with me in prayer.

Let us converse with the KING.

not able to be changed, reversed, or
recovered; final.

I Bow

As I Bless...

Decrees

As I bless the Lord I am put into remembrance of HIS grace.
As I bless the Lord I am put it in remembrance of all HIS power.
As I bless the Lord I am put into remembrance of HIS recompense.
As I bless the Lord I am put into remembrance of HIS reward.
As I bless the Lord I am putting to remembrance of HIS good acts toward me.
As I bless the Lord I am put into remembrance of the Requital.
As I bless the Lord I am put into remembrance of HIS love.
As I bless the Lord I am convinced HE is for me.
As I bless the Lord I am convinced HE is with me.
As I bless the Lord I am convinced that HE is remembering me.
As I bless the Lord I am convinced of HIS character.
As I bless the Lord I am convinced that HIS word is my truth.
As I bless the Lord I am convinced my day is already blessed
As I bless the Lord I am convinced the field of my labor is already blessed.
As I bless the Lord I am convinced my worship works.
As I bless the Lord I am convinced prayer works.
As I bless the Lord I am convinced my fasting works.
As I bless the Lord I am convinced he hears me when I pray.
As I bless the Lord I am convinced that no ill will comes my way.
As I bless the Lord all deception flees from his presence.
As I bless the Lord I am convinced I walk in joy.
As I bless the Lord I am convinced that HE enjoys my worship.
As I bless the Lord I am convinced that HE enjoys my prayers.
As I bless the Lord I am convinced HE is rewarding my intercession.
As I bless the Lord I am convinced HIS presence hangs around me
As I bless the Lord I am convinced light only surrounds me as HE is the 'Father of Light'.
As I bless the Lord I am convinced the darkness cannot come near my dwelling place.

As I bless the Lord I remember that I abide the secret place of the almighty

As I bless the Lord I am put into remembrance that under HIS shadow is where I dwell.

As I bless the Lord I remember that I will not be put into fear by the things I see as I go out to my day.

As I bless the Lord my soul leaps.

As I bless the Lord I am put into remembrance of how powerful my worship is.

As I bless the LORD my soul is me glad.

As I bless the LORD I go in peace.

As I bless the LORD I remember how amazing HE IS.

As I bless the LORD I remember I love being alive.

As I bless the LORD I understand my life counts.

As I bless the LORD I am motivated to get out and live.

As I bless the LORD I am energized to go live.

As I bless the LORD I understand my life blesses HIM with me.

As I bless the LORD my life fights for the promises with me.

AS I bless the LORD obedience is a benefit.

As I bless the LORD my hands are strengthened to do the work.

As I bless the LORD my work blesses HIM too.

As I bless the LORD my attitude aligns with the promised outcomes.

As I bless the LORD...I win.

I won.

I will keep winning because HE has given me the key to HIS Presence.

Worship.

As I bless the LORD!

The Call

Decree

GOD has forgiven me.
God has released me.
God has pardoned me.
God has spared me.
God has judged me favorably.
God has received me.
God calls me holy.
God calls me acceptable.
God calls me son/daughter.
God calls me into his presence.
God calls me righteousness or in right-standing with him.
God calls me free.
God calls me by name.
GOD calls me HIS.

GOD called me even when I was not answering HIM.
GOD called me even when I did not want to be called.
GOD strived with me even when I shunned HIM.
GOD paid attention to me even when I ignored HIM.
GOD friended me when I was an enemy to HIM.

GOD loved me before I even loved me. *ALL*, every iota, every particle of iniquity, guilt of iniquity, the guilt of conditions, every consequence related to perversity, depravity, and iniquity has been eradicated from my past, present and future.

I denounce the past iniquities and their associated consequences. I will not be shamed into false consequences for ***passed*** history. ***Passed*** as in dead, ***passed*** as in eulogized, ***passed*** and in dead and buried, ***passed*** as in murdered, ***passed*** as in buried in the cemetery never to be dug up. Never to be made alive again, never to be named amongst my members again, never to be named among the names of my children and their members.
BE FORE GAVE YOU Christ

Prayer

Father, I admit, I have no idea how to comprehend your *LOVE*. I admit your love is like nothing that I ever experienced. I admit, I want to love you like you love me—but I don't have the capacity to. I am striving to worship you properly. I admit, I do not know how to worship you... I admit I do not know how to pray as I ought to but here again you make a way for me.

I admit. I have a definition but it is NOT the full definition of my experience with you.

So in the name of Jesus—my hope, my light and my filling—I pray, and praise past my intellect. I pray into what I do not understand. I pray INTO the promises ALREADY full and released over my life. I decree into...I decide every WORD of GOD is for me.

EVERY miracle of GOD is for me. EVERY breath of GOD blows over me... Every angel sent, every angel assigned charge over me to bear me up is FOR me. I decide, and decree I do not need to fully understand to receive it. I do not need to fully understand to live it. I do not need to fully understand it...I do not understand the sun, moon, and stars—how they were made, what they are made out of, how they stick and stay where they are for all these years yet, I still benefit from what I do not understand. I apply this same principles and HOLY analytics to what I do not understand about how YOU are with me, who YOU are with me, and why YOU are with me. I do not need to comprehend NOW I just need to receive NOW; all other things will fall into place.

As I worship my way into the deeper depths of the mysteries of HIM—I understand. I stand under the open heavens of his love and care for me. The hardships I endured were to build me not break me. I am not broken. I was built for 'Grace-tough'.

I stand under an open heaven of benefits only. I stand under an open heaven of healing only--*ONLY healing*. There is healing in my very DNA. My allegiance to GOD. JESUS activates the power, miracles, healing, which are already present within me. The domain of GOD—the rule of GOD—the will of GOD—already INSIDE me. Already working for me. Greater is HE that is in me... all that HE is in me. HIS character, the power of his name, the person and the power of HIS presence are in IN ME. I decide to accept and receive it. I decide to walk in it. I decide to work in it. I decide this is my portion...I decide this is for ME. THIS IS MY TESTIMONY. It is established.

THIS Truth...THIS IS MY TRUTH.

This truth begins to activate the healing from every disease, illness, sickness, ill health; infection, ailment, malady, disorder, complaint, affliction, condition, indisposition, upset, problem, trouble, infirmity, disability, defect, abnormality; pestilence, plague, cancer, canker, blight; informal bug, virus; dated contagion that would exist in the seen or the unseen... that which exists in the spiritual and the natural. Every ailment in every facet of my existence is eradicated, declared improper and unlawful in relation to the domain of GOD in ME and the domain of GOD I reside in.

The truth relieves me of every discomfort associated with the aforementioned diseases—discomforts as: embarrassment, discomfiture, unease, uneasiness, awkwardness, discomposure, confusion, nervousness, perturbation, distress, anxiety; lack of physical comfort. Every inconvenience, difficulty, bother, nuisance, vexation, drawback, disadvantage, trouble, problem, trial, tribulation, hardship; informal hassle I reject you now, I eject you know, I disassociate with you...no thank you, I don't want you, I do not receive you, I do not EXPECT you, I do not welcome you...I reject you in every sense of the WORD of GOD in the name of JESUS.

I am healed by the standard of the definition uttered by the ONE who created healing. MY healing worships the Creator. MY healing bows before GOD and performs the GOOD pleasure of GOD in every dimension of MY existence.

With all confidence I say, "IN YOU I LIVE. IN YOU I MOVE. IN YOU I HAVE MY VERY BEING. IN YOU I WORSHIP. IN YOU I AM WHOLE. IN YOU I AM FREE. IN YOU I EXPRESS YOU IN YOU. I ENCOUNTER YOU, IN YOU....IN YOU...I AM IN YOU. YOU ARE IN ME."

JEHOVAH MY FREEDOM!!!!!

Ransom

Prayer

Father, I pray into the ransomed price you payed for my wholeness and my freedom. I am no longer in exile; I am no longer an outsider to the precious promises—but I am an insider. My life is no longer on the path of destruction. Everything in the realm and territory of my life is on the path of freedom and open space. There are no longer any traps, destruction, ditches, pits, holes, hidden snares, foul fowlers, obstructions, hindrances, graves, pits of hell, damages, demolition teams, demolition plots, annihilations, eliminations, eradications, liquidations, derailments—the plot for my ruin has been overturned as the gavel bangs the HOLY Podium in the Courts of Heaven.

Decree

That's right. The judgement is in my favor. That's right there is restitution for the years of struggle and hidden traps for my life. That's right my sins and transgressions have been dismissed. DISMISSED in the court of HEAVEN by the Holiest of Holiest...GOD my great judge.
Now in the place of destruction there is a CROWN of life placed upon my head. There is a crown of kindness and tender mercies placed upon my head and the head of my life. My life is crowned with kindness and tender mercies.

My life has been crowned with beauty, favor, good deeds, mercy, pity, affection, concern, care, warm-heartedness, thoughtfulness, compassion, understanding, generosity, friendliness, magnanimity, hospitality, charitableness, big-heartedness, accommodation, help, assistance, special favor, and aid. I am forgiven, I have received complete clemency. I have received holy forbearance. I have received blessing. I have received a windfall of GOD. I have received a windfall of GOD from GOD. Just as the sound as the gavel banging upon the Judge's bench in the heavens the sound reverberates in the earth over me and in me. The decision has been made and it is forever. The decision over me is irreversible. The decision over me is until the Day of Jesus. The decision over me is impenetrable.

My life, to include everything seen and unseen. My life to include everything past, everything in the present, and everything in the future. My life to include my spirit, my soul, and my flesh. My life to include the generations before me, the generations of now, and the generations to come. My life is satisfied by GOD. GOD is the one who has given me plenty. GOD is the one, that has caused me to be full, GOD is the one to have caused my cup to be over-flowing. I am satisfied. I am sated, I am fulfilled, I am in excess, I am surfeited, I am enriched, I am bursting at the seams with the GOOD things of GOD. The good things of GOD are mine.

Every good thing that is gracious, kind, joyous, merry, pleasant, precious, loving merry, sweet, prosperous, wealth, welfare of favor, agreeable, of high nature, valuable in estimation, appropriate to the standard of CHRIST, becoming as in beauty, glad, and in good standing—ethical, benefitting, morally good, causing happiness, and bountiful.

The GOOD of GOD has given me back my child-like faith. The GOOD of GOD has caused me to have the joy of school children. The good of GOD has reversed all signs of aging in my spirit, my mind, my thoughts, my behaviors, my skin, my organs, my muscles, my brain, my emotions, my relationships, my cognitive abilities, my memory, my playfulness, my flexibility, my imagination, my amazement, my ability to love, my ability to forgive, my desire to live, my desire to serve. JESUS CHRIST is the renewal of my existence. The Law of First Mentions is working in my life. The first time GOD mentioned me in the heavens—how my life was to look before HIM, how my life was to playout in the earth. The First Mentions of my name by HIM is alive and well! This is the inner-workings and outer-workings for my life. I have been renewed. This is the only option over me.

I am like the eagle. I am renewed to power, I am renewed to strength, I am renewed to joy, I am renewed to peace, I am renewed IN favor, I am renewed in strength, I am renewed in anointing, I am renewed before my friends and before my foes. My renewal is untouchable. My renewal is being continuously renewed in the secret place. My renewal is lasting. My renewal is everlasting. My renewal is eternal. My renewal is IN CHRIST. I am renewed. I am new. I am again new. In Jesus name

GOD thank you for executing righteous acts. Eternal GOD, Self-existent GOD thank YOU for executing judgement in favor of all that are oppressed. Thank you for accomplishing, advancing, appointing, beating, bestowing, and bringing forth, charging, executing, exercise, feasting, finishing, fulfilling, gathering hindering, holding, keeping, laboring, maintaining, observing, paring bringing to pass, performing, praising, preparing procuring providing, putting, requiting, sacrificing, serving, setting, showing sinning, spending, taking, trimming, warring working all righteous acts and judgements.

Deliverer

Prayer

Father thank you, that your expectation over me and my life mirrors that of Moses.

The name Moses means "drawing out of water" the "rescued". The same way you drew him out of the waters of destruction and planted him in particular era where he was assigned to be the deliverer. I am thankful GOD that I do not know all your plans but I can look at your pattern and trace your goodness toward me. I believe, Father, that where I have been in my past, the places I tripped through, the places that almost captured me--these places never actually had any type of hold on me. I honor you GOD, that I can plainly see the deliverer portion upon my head. I can see the mandate of the rescuer in me because you have rescued me over and over and over again.

I believe that as I bless you—you are going to reveal the paths of righteousness for my life. I believe you are going to release the blueprints of heaven. I believe that you are not holding back any good thing from me. I believe that you are revealing the mysterious of your domain unto me. I believe that I have power of the Pharaohs of the land. I believe that systems of domination that have held your people captive are coming down at the treading of my feet. I believe I am the sound of the proclamation of peace, the trumpet blast of freedom blows through me and my life. I Receive the sound of heaven, I receive the hedges and hedging of heaven, I receive the untouchable status that comes upon my life I say a resounding YES to YOU in this place of wisdom and this place of worship. YOU are my help...YOU are the help for the people. I ride the waves of your spirit and I command my soul to get on board and arise to the challenge.

Decree

I like David, perceive now is the time to respond. Now is the time to respond whole heartedly and to take up the sword of authority which is the Word of YOU. I admit I am the man/woman for the job. I admit that I am mandated to go thru these waters. I come into agreement with the portions of power, and anointing needed to get this job down. I am well able. I am well able because YOU have strengthened me. IN the end of it all GOD—YOU are still Jehovah my HERO. Hero of the nations, hero of the peoples, hero of the universe, you are the hero...
I bless YOU as HERO GOD, Champion GOD, Winner-GOD, Triumphant GOD!!!!!!

AS I bless YOU, chains are being lifted, broken and yokes are being destroyed. As I bless YOU systems are weakening before the very power of the loving GOD. AS I bless YOU—YOU are stirring yourself upon your throne. As I bless YOU the nations tremble. As I bless YOU the peoples tremble. As I bless YOU the captive is being led away captive. I was built for this because I said I would go for YOU before YOU formed me—I already said YES. My answer is still yes. My answer is still yes. My answer is still yes!!!!!!!! Yes, now and yes forever!!!!!!!
Ancient of Days hear and receive my words of covenant as I address YOU as KING and LORD!

Jehovah Is Mine

Decree

I decide and choose today to put on display the names of GOD—
describing how he has showing up for me over and over and over.

I call GOD—Merciful One, Compassionate companion, Loving Ruler,
Sweet Lord, Kind Keeper, Charitable Champion, Empathetically
Involved One, Gracious GOD, Sympathetic KING, Charitable GOD,
Softhearted Elohim, Creative GOD, Miracle Giving GOD, Favor-
extending Father.

The Lord my GOD is the keeper of his Promises.
The Lord my GOD is the Keeper of Covenants.
The lord my GOD is the Keeper of Oaths.
The Lord my GOD is solid in nature.
The lord my GOD is Champion of All.
The Lord my GOD remembers and recalls my frailty.
The Lord my GOD makes room for me daily.
The Lord my GOD calls me daily.
The Lord my GOD is with me always.
The Lord my GOD keeps my frame.
The lord my god is patient.
The lord my GOD strives with me.
The lord my GOD is quick to forgive me.
The Lord my GOD is quick to act on my behalf.
The Lord my GOD extends power toward me.
The Lord my GOD thinks GOD thoughts toward me constantly.
The Lord my GOD guides me continually.
The Lord my GOD keeps my foot from falling.
The Lord my GOD assigned angels to me.
The Lord my GOD assigned goodness and mercy to me.
The Lord my GOD causes me to rest.
The Lord my GOD causes me to be in peace.
The Lord my GOD is perfect in ALL HIS ways.
The Lord my is GOOD in all HIS ways.

The Lord my GOD has no evil intent in HIM.
The Lord my GOD is not keeping anything from me.
The Lord my GOD is causing all goodness to pass before me.
The LORD my GOD honors me.
The Lord my GOD reveals secrets to me.
The Lord my GOD unravels the universe for me.
The Lord my GOD causes my enemy to be scattered.
The Lord my GOD causes my boarders to be impenetrable.
The LORD my GOD raises me up for low places.
The Lord my GOD helps me.
The Lord my GOD calms me.
The Lord my GOD watches over my soul.
The Lord my GOD is my great KING.
The lord my GOD is my Great Shepard.
The Lord my GOD is my Great Reward.
The Lord my GOD is the Object of my affection.
The LORD my GOD makes me the object his affection.
The Lord my GOD loves to bless me.
The Lord my GOD causes me to ride the wind of HIS benefits.
The lord my GOD breaks up the fallow ground before me.
The lord my GOD plants me in pleasant gardens.
The Lord my GOD causes my life to produce GOD fruit.
The Lord my GOD shifts winds to favor me.
The LORd my GOD keeps records of my righteousness only.
The Lord my GOD causes me to fall in love with him over and over and over.
The Lord my GOD strengthens my courage.
The Lord my GOD causes me to sing a new sound of 'winfare'.
The Lord my GOD causes my feet to be like hinds' feet.
The lord my GOD causes my life to dance.
The lord my GOD causes my life to drip with sweetness.
The lord my GOD causes my life to eat the Fat of the land.
The Lord my GOD causes me to arise and shine.
The Lord my GOD causes oil to drip from my eyes.
The Lord my GOD causes me to run through troops.
The Lord my GOD causes my mouth to prophesy.

The Lord my GOD robes me in majesty.
The Lord my GOD mantles me in purpose.
The Lord my GOD causes my transitions to move with grace.
The Lord my GOD calms the wind and the waves in my life.
The Lord is my GOD.
Jehovah is my Everything.
Jehovah is my life.
Jehovah is my goodness.
Jehovah is my light.
Jehovah is my substance.
Jehovah is my ROCK.
Jehovah is my hope.
Jehovah is my faith.
Jehovah is my *IRREVOCABLE DECREE*.

278 ametamélē tos

properly, no change of concern (interest), i.e. *without regret or remorse* for an action because it was done from *deep conviction* (true concern).

Reverene The Lord

Decree

MY Jehovah holds no aught with me. The war has ended. The controversy has ended. Never to be recalled or rehashed. The contending, wrangling, complaint, rebuke and chiding has ended. GOD is not out to get me. GOD is not lying in wait to destroy me. GOD is on my side. GOD loves me to no end. GOD is not angry with me. GOD is not angry with me. GOD is not ignoring my voice. GOD is not turning away from me. GOD does not label me as evil but as the righteousness of HIMSELF through Christ Jesus. I receive the GOD-labels. I receive the GOD-naming. I receive the God-status.

GOD has not dealt with me according to my sin.
GOD has not awarded me what I truly deserved.
GOD has not accomplished, advanced, bestowed, brought forth, committed, dealt, executed, fitted, furnished granted, governed, observed, performed, pronounced, requited, spent, pressed, or squeezed my life, my person, according to the measure of my seed of sin. GOD is not fair. GOD is just but he is not fair. I came out on the greater side of my sin. I came out unscathed in relation to what should have been poured into my life. The crimes I committed, the offences I constructed, the mischief I danced in—GOD LET ME GO! GOD did not allow the ripening of sins fruit to bloom or blossom. GOD allowed there to be no damage beyond repair. GOD dealt with me with the hand of LOVE. GOD dealt with me through the lens of acknowledging HIS dear SON.

I am ok.
I am free.
I walked out of sin intact.
GOD preserved me.

103:11

Decree

As I reverence the LORD.
AS I YARE (YAW-RAY, 03373)
AS I revere THE LORD.
AS I stand in awe of the LORD.
AS I honor the LORD.
AS I respect the LORD.
AS I am astonished by the LORD.
AS I am held in AWE of the LORD.
AS I acclaim the LORD.
AS I appreciate the LORD.
AS I Hold high estimation of the LORD.
AS I have high regard for the LORD.
AS I RESPECT the LORD.
AS I offer obsequie of the LORD.
AS I prostrate before the LORD
AS I deify the LORD.
AS I BOW to the LORD.
As I show veneration to the LORD.
AS I am in WONDER of the LORD.
AS I am sincere before the LORD
AS I am passionate before the LORD.
AS I am regardful toward the LORD.
AS I show deference to the LORD.
AS I exalt the LORD...

SO great HIS mercy bends toward me.
SO great HIS favor bends toward me.
SO great HIS wholeness bends toward me.
SO great HIS healthiness bends toward me.
SO great HIS wealth bends toward me.
SO great HIS fruit drops before me.
SO great HIS HEAVEN open over me.
SO great HIS doors open unto me.

SO great HIS NAME performs for me.
SO great HIS word manifest for me.
SO great HIS hand wars for me.
SO great HIS power HIS influences me.
SO great HIS wisdom washes over me.
SO great HIS anointing responds in me.
SO great HIS purpose flows out of me.
SO great HIS presence surrounds me.
SO great HIS awesomeness floods me

AS high as the heaven is high above the earth so GREAT all these benefits and more that my mouth cannot contain are bending toward me and showing me favor. MY life is favored. These attributes are the standard for my life. These attributes of GOD are the base of my existence. This is the only confession that I decide is my portion and that of my family.

SO great is my LIFE in JESUS.
Thank you JESUS.
Thank you LORD for my new life in you.
Jesus is my life.

Racham: Compassion

I am safe

Prayer

Father, in the name of Christ, I resolve to repent and relent concerning myself in regards to how you view me. I understand that when I received Christ the eternal war ended. I am no longer in war with you. I am no longer at war with myself. I release myself from all of the sin and evil that I have engaged in over the span of my lifetime. I now announce to myself, I announce to my soul, I announce to my heart that I am free.

As far are the east is from the west, as far as the left is from the right, and up is from down—so is the evil doings of my past from the righteousness of my present. My transgressions have been removed from me. The stain has been removed from me. The scar of transgression has been sent far away from my spiritual person as well as my natural person. The sin and scars of my past and sins and scars from my lineage have been erased. I shall not behold any chokeholds of the evil upon my generations. I have been loosed and therefore my lineage has been loosed. My old sin-self has wandered into the captivity of the stronghold of GOD and my new nature has been released to upon me and released upon my lineage.

Decree

GOD took pity on me—He gave me JESUS.
The pity of GOD is the favor of GOD.
The pity of GOD out the "racham" of GOD is to be loved deeply, to have tender affection, and compassion lavished on me.
Christ has been lavished upon me.

Holy Spirit has been lavished upon me. I receive the pity of GOD. God lavished my with love because I revere him, because I stand in awe of HIM. Not because I work hard. Not because I pray hard. Not because I am perfect…. but rather because I stand in awe of HIM. The more I revere HIM…greater amounts of the lavish love of GOD becomes tangible to me. I am living in the pity of GOD. I am living in Christ. I am living in the lavish love of GOD and today I stop and relish in the moment (s) and person of GOD's pity.

Christ the LORD.

The Racham of GOD will never run out. The racham of GOD will never be turned from me. The racham of GOD was present even while I was deep in sin. The racham of GOD was there the whole time patiently waiting to embrace me.

GOD created me, GOD formed me my frame. GOD remembers that I am earth and I am dirt in my natural self—but he extends his PITY and allows me to walk in the supernatural pattern and purpose of HIS destiny toward me.

I pray into the prophetic destiny of YOU GOD. I pray into the blessing hanging over you GOD—the picture of me being free to perform the will in the earth that you have performed in me through the pity you bestowed upon me. I receive the prophetic destiny of heaven and my role in this destiny coming upon the earth and mankind.

The days of man are short but the days of the spirit of man are eternal. I walk not according to the brevity of the life span of mortality. Rather, I put on the armor of the eternal decision of GOD concerning me.

I walk according to the prophetic destiny of the eternal favor of GOD to be with HIM.

The prosperity of temporary things no longer tempts me away from the eternal destiny with the Father. Rather, I buy into the mercy and the pity of GOD which Is from everlasting to everlasting. I am living in the everlasting of GOD now.

I have put away the nature of myself that would fall back into a place of unbelief. Unbelief of HIM seeing me through the purity of HIS SON. I am pure and because I exist in the purity of Christ from everlasting to everlasting. The moments that I find myself slipping into wrong doing the everlasting mercy covenant is in full activation mode over my prophetic destiny.

The mercy of GOD is from everlasting to everlasting because I revere Him. AS I stand in awe of GOD righteousness—justice, righteousness of government, righteousness of GOD's attributes, righteousness is case or cause, righteousness in truthfulness, righteousness in what is ethically right, righteousness as what is vindicated justified, and salvation of GOD, and the prosperity of people is effected toward my children's children.
My seed is under the covenant of everlasting mercy and everlasting righteousness!

I keep the covenants of GOD and I do them.

I walk away from all patterns within myself accusing me of not being weighty enough to carry this everlasting glory and everlasting mercy. I release myself from taking on the futile task with finite ability to do this isolated from the goodness of GOD.

GOD decided this was my portion.
God called me into the realms and depths of glory-catching and glory-carrying.
I decree the 'irrevocable decree' GOD makes this a sweat-less victory for me to keep HIM.

His covenants are HIM...**I revere HIM so I keep HIM**. Because I decide TODAY that GOD is for me in this walk— the covenant is being established. The covenant of KEEPING HIM is being deeply rooted in my life and in my lineage. The covenant of GOD is written upon my DNA and written in my DNA. I am awakened and alerted to the AWE of the covenant. The AWE of the Testimony of Christ as being my DNA. This is what I am made of.

HE keeps me; I keep HIM.

The Irrevocable Decree

The Word Is...

The Lord has prepared his throne in the heavens; and his kingdom rules over all.

The Lord has ordained, established, fashioned, made-ready, framed, confirmed, caused to be enduring, caused to be securely determined, arranged, settled, accomplished, and furnished HIS seat of honor, seat of royal dignity, seat of authority, and seat of power in the visible sky and the abode of GOD; and HIS rule, dominion, sovereign power, and royalty is fixed, securely determined, steadfast, and established over all.

The LORD cannot be moved. The reign of GOD cannot be removed. The victory I have in GOD cannot be penetrated in the earth or in the heavens. The throne of GOD and the domain OF GOD is firmly established in me and over me as I move in the constraints of the freedom of Christ. The plumb line of GLORY is fixed over my days. The ruler-ship and authorship of the KING has written my books. I am moving in the finished works and established IRREVOCABLE Decree of GOD.

I am walking out the momentous momentum of eternity moments in the minutes of my natural life.

GOD is ruling over me.
Everything that pertains to me is fixed under the ruler-ship of the throne of GOD. I submit to the framework that is established. I just submit. I sit under the OPEN portals constructed by, and constructed for the reign, and rains of GOD.
The domain of GOD is my home.
The domain of GOD is my structure.
The domain of GOD is sanctuary.
I run in and I am safe, I am saved, and I am sozo.

Bless the LORD you his angels, that excel in strength, that do his commandments, hearkening to the voice of his word.

Barak the LORD, kneel, praise and salute the LORD you his ministers, messengers, deputies, dispatched to do HIS bidding in my life and the bidding in the earth. I declare to you angelic deputies that you are excelling in power, excelling in bravery, excelling in might as you bear, bestow, advance, bring forth, follow further gather, grant, garner, hinder, hold, perform, prepare, labor, maintain, journey, keep, go about, govern, execute and exercise HIS oracles, speech, word, utterances, business matters, cases, tidings, chronicles, glory, pleasure, songs, tasks and HIS WHATSOEVERS! The angelic deputies hear, listen and obey with attention and interest unto the voice, sound, lightness, spark, song, thunder of HIS words, decrees, songs, sounds, purpose, matters, speech, utterances, business, acts, matters, tasks, reports, judgements, duties, and ***IRREVOCABLE DECREES***.

Bless ye the LORD, all ye HIS hosts, ye ministers of HIS that do HIS pleasure.

Barak—kneel, praise, and salute the Eternal GOD, all of HIS assembled to go out and do battle. Host of the organized spiritual army, host of the angels, army of whole creation. Every trained solider designed to battle in this dispensation of time in all of creation I call you into the order of GOD. As you fight for HIM you are saluting HIM. Host of all creation as you do battle for my prophetic destiny you are saluting the KING. Every atom, particle of dirt and air, all vegetation, every species I call into the position of saluting the KING by warring on my behalf. I call into order every battle warrior that is called to this victory for this time. Every host in the heavens and in the earth...every general, every captain within the perimeters of creation COME NOW, HEED NOW, WAR NOW, ASSEMBLE and move into position.

𝕭less the Lord all HIS works in all places of HIS dominion. 𝕭less the Lord, O my soul.

Barak, kneel and bless the LORD all works in all places.

Every deed in earth bless the Lord.
Everything done in the earth Bless the Lord.
Every Act in earth bless the Lord.
Every labor in the earth bless the Lord.
Every labor in the earth bless the Lord.
Every business in the earth bless the Lord.
Every pursuit in the earth bless the Lord.
Every undertaking in the earth bless the Lord.
Every enterprise in the earth bless the Lord.
Every achievement in the earth bless the Lord.
Every work of deliverance in the earth bless the Lord.
Every word of GOD in the earth bless the Lord.
Every product in the earth bless the Lord.

Bless the LORD all the works in all place in the earth under the reign and domain of GOD. Everything, and I declare everything is under the ruler-ship of GOD. GOD is the power of my life. GOD has dominion in all places that my feet tread. GOD has complete dominion of my whole existence. I dedicate everything put under my ruler-ship and dominion-ship under HIM. I move in the freedom of HIS completeness.

This day, right now—I totally and utterly hand over my existence to the KING of KINGS.

I vow before the Master this day—my soul's purpose is to bless you. GOD, I was built to bless you. My spirit, soul, and body all belong to you. Father, I am asking for you to remake and reshape me for my destiny. I bow along with the totality of all things in me and connected to me toward you. I partner with you GOD.

I partner with your will as I prostrate in belief.

I struggle no more with the command toward me. I struggle no more with the work before me. I struggle no more with the past that has passed from me. I honor the places I have been afforded to adventure with you. I am renewed in your word. YOUR word toward me is the building blocks of my life. I no longer hesitate at YOUR word. Right now I decide your word it is for me.
AS I bless YOU, I believe the power of your promise comes upon me because YOU are able to perform it.

GOD seals these declarations with the signet ring of GOD. I have opened my mouth and declared an irrevocable decree. Everything in the earth along with everything under the earth; now, hear and obey the WORD of the LORD. I participate, model, verbalize, and activate the GOD-breathed truths HE has declared over me. I honor the covenant of HIS heart for me through the HIS WORD.

IT IS FINISHED.
Selah.

As I bless the LORD.

I shall see you in the dimensions of prayer.
Until we meet again.
Keep praying.
Keep worshipping.
Keep winning.

In HIS love,
Annice Silimon
www.annicesilimon.com
annice@annicesilimon.com

Made in the USA
Middletown, DE
07 February 2019